TRIPLE WHAMMY

TO SIDO AND JONAS

Triple Whammy
Copyright © 1993 by Teryl Euvremer
Printed in the U.S.A. All rights reserved.
Typography by Al Cetta
1 2 3 4 5 6 7 8 9 10 ❖
First Edition

Library of Congress Cataloging-in-Publication Data
Euvremer, Teryl.
    Triple whammy / Teryl Euvremer.
        p.   cm.
    Summary: A monster and a witch grow bored with their marriage when they run out
of ways to be mean to each other, until they transform themselves into various
interesting creatures.
    ISBN 0-06-021060-5. — ISBN 0-06-021061-3 (lib. bdg.)
    [1. Monsters—Fiction. 2. Witches—Fiction. 3. Invective—Fiction. 4. Humorous
stories.] I. Title.
PZ7.E8735Tr 1993   91-44240
[E]—dc20   CIP
                                                                      AC

TRIPLE WHAMMY

TERYL EUVREMER

HarperCollins*Publishers*

Blavia and Mug lived in a faraway corner of the earth where no one ever ventured.

Mug was a monster.
Blavia was a witch.

Monsters and witches
always marry
someone they despise.

Mug and Blavia whiled away the time giving each other the triple whammy, playing foul, and fighting dirty. A withering look from Blavia was very unpleasant. Mug's heartlessness knew no bounds.

And the nasty things they said to each other could make your ears fall off.

There was just one thing over which they could see
eye to eye. Mug and Blavia shared a passion for
the same book.

All of the creatures they had never seen leaped, slid, flew,
and crawled through its pages.

One picture showed a pair of human beings.
"Nothing interesting about those," said Mug. "No fangs, no
claws, wet squinty eyes . . ."

"And that sappy smile," said Blavia. "Horrible!
Turn the page!"

Mug and Blavia's life
together continued
in this hot-blooded way until,
one day,

they could think
of no new pranks
to play.

Blavia's withering look
no longer shriveled Mug.
Mug's heartlessness
left Blavia cold.
Blavia and Mug were bored.

"Stop staring at the ceiling and DO something,
you washed-out quagmire of a crocodile," said Blavia.
"Look who's talking," yawned Mug. "Stop lying there
glued to the table like a lollygagging slug."

"If I *were* a slug," retorted Blavia, perking up, "I would slide
across your repellent crocodile mug
and leave a sticky trail of goo. . . ."
"Just you try it!" said Mug.

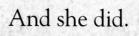

And she did.

The new game continued all morning.
"Overturned footstool of a turtle!"
said Blavia.
"Garbage-guzzling gabberlunzie
of a goose!" said Mug.

The new game continued all day.
"You obsolete oversized eyesore!" said Blavia.
"You dinosaur!"

"You clothespin-clawed
crustacean!" said Mug.
"You crab!"

The game continued all week.
"Take that, you mop-legged octopus!" said Mug.
"Take that, you gaudy flapdoodle of a butterfly!"
said Blavia.

All month.
"Ragtag, stubble-chinned
hyena!" said Blavia.
"Obnoxious, nictitating
nightmare of a toad!"
said Mug.

Two hundred years later, they were still at it.
"I'm choosing today," said Mug, thumbing through
their precious book.
"Not on your horny hide," said Blavia. "You're capable
of turning us into some spiritless specimens like these."
Blavia pointed to one of the pictures.
"Is that a dare?" asked Mug.

And in less time than it takes to say "You're IT!"
Mug and Blavia became . . . *Homo sapiens*. People.
Man and Woman.

Mug's new smile was sweet. Blavia bashfully lowered
her eyelids. Their hearts throbbed like harmoniums
in their neat human bodies.

Soon other creatures began to appear.

Mug and Blavia were
never bored again.